The Kids' Book of Questions

NEW EDITION

Gregory Stock, Ph.D.

Workman Publishing • New York

Copyright © 1988, 2004 by Gregory Stock

Library of Congress Cataloging-in-Publication Data is available.

ISBN 0-7611-3595-2

Cover illustration by Paul Anderson

Workman Publishing Company, Inc.
708 Broadway
New York, NY 10003-9555
www.workman.com

Printed in U.S.A.

First printing October 2004

10 9 8 7 6 5 4 3 2 1

To Sadie, the princess of my heart.

To Ben the king, Aliza the queen, and
Paul, Miranda, Liffie, Kippie, Zach,
Scott, Sam, Ben, and Jake the
minnow catcher.

Acknowledgments

For their ideas, suggestions, and encouragement, I particularly thank Lillian McKinstry and Donald Ponturo. For her love and support, I thank Lori Fish. And I thank Douglas Balfour, Joseph Cambray, Kenny Cleveland, Sheila Garrigue, Jason Ide, Nettie Ide, Katy Fassett, Jane Stock, Jason Sullivan, Daniel Summer, Claudia Summer, Fred Weber, and the Denver Children's Museum.

For editorial assistance as well as ideas and suggestions, I thank Michael Cader and David Allender.

Introduction

Most of the questions you are asked at school have right and wrong answers: Who invented the steam engine? What is the capital of Italy? How is blue cheese made? Such questions have answers you can always find in books or on the Internet, so it doesn't really matter if you sometimes don't know the answers.

The questions here do not have answers you can find in such places because they are about you. Knowing what you believe in and who you are is very important, so look into yourself to find answers to these questions. This is not a test, though; no one answer is right for everyone. Here, there are no correct answers—only honest ones—and you are the only one who really knows how honest you are being. Don't say what you think others want you to; respond the way you actually feel.

The Kids' Book of Questions is for kids, but it is not a book of childish questions. Some questions are playful, even downright silly. Others are serious and focus upon the hard dilemmas you face in growing up. They raise issues about dealing with authority, understanding friendship, handling social pressures, overcoming fears, and deciding what's right and wrong. You will face these issues throughout your life.

Growing up is not easy these days. Kids are not sheltered from divorce, crime, drugs, sex, violence, and other things that are hard even for adults to deal with. You get a lot of advice from your family, friends, teachers, and even from television and movies; but different people will tell you different things about what you should and shouldn't do. What is right? Where do you fit into the world? Who can you trust? A big part of growing up is learning to make choices for yourself.

Thinking about questions like the ones in this book is a good way of practicing to do just that. When you use your imagination to explore difficult dilemmas, you can learn from situations without going through them in real life. So throw yourself into these questions and pretend they're real. When you care about a decision, the process of deciding will bring you new thoughts, ideas, and opinions that are entirely your own. Take this chance to discuss the things you feel most strongly about instead of everyday matters you've already talked about dozens of times.

With some of these questions you have to pretend you have extraordinary powers or are in strange and unusual situations. With others, you must remember your past or imagine your future. Treat these questions as your own. Play with them, add to them, change them, but don't cheat by trying to figure out ways to keep from having to make hard choices, because you will only be cheating yourself. And don't just answer yes or no—or let others get away with that. Try to figure out why you feel the way you do, and push others to do the same, because the reasons behind people's answers are often even more interesting than the answers themselves.

Playing with questions like these is a game to laugh and have fun with. It can also be a bit uncomfortable, because sometimes it is not easy to look at yourself and think about the kind of person you are, what you want, and what you care about. Talking about your thoughts and feelings with your friends will be a big help when you face difficult and confusing questions in this book, and when you next face tough choices in the real world. Just remember that growing occurs not from having answers but from searching for them.

A big difference between questions about things and questions about people is that you are never quite sure where personal questions will lead. Maybe that is why personal questions are so much fun. This book gives you an easy, playful way of raising issues you've wanted to talk about but haven't known how to bring up. Make full use of the chance and use these questions by yourself, with your friends, or even with adults.

Start asking the questions you find here, and similar questions of your own, and you'll soon be having lively discussions. I hope this new edition helps you see how sweet it can be to ask thought-provoking questions. It is amazing where one little question can take you. Good luck and have fun.

1

If you ruled the world and could have anything you wanted, and people would do anything you wanted, do you think you'd get greedy and mean or be good and fair?

2

Do you think boys or girls have it easier?

3

If your mother promised to be home at 2:00 in the afternoon to take you to the movies but didn't show up until suppertime and didn't even phone, what would be a good punishment for her? Would punishing her be likely to make her be on time in the future?

4

If all your best friends were willing to be absolutely honest and tell you exactly what they most liked and disliked about you, would you want them to?

5

Would you rather have a strict teacher who was fair and taught you a lot or one who was relaxed and fun but didn't teach you much?

6

One day your father gets a really weird idea and dyes his hair green and puts a ring through his nose. Knowing everyone would be looking at him and snickering, would you go shopping with him if he wanted your company?

7

When you make a mistake, do you make up excuses? If so, do you think people believe you?

8

If you could have a round-trip ride in a time machine and travel any distance into the past or future, where would you want to go?

9

If a friend had an important secret and didn't want other people to learn about it, would telling you the secret be a big mistake?

10

If your parents were worried about a serious problem that had nothing to do with you directly, would you want them to tell you about it or would you rather not know?

11

What would you do if everyone in your family forgot your birthday?

12

How would you act differently if you had a younger sister who idolized you and tried to copy everything you did? What things do you think your parents do only because they want to set an example for you? Do you think they have done things they won't tell you about because they're worried you might try to copy them?

13

If you were alone and had only a few minutes to hide from crooks who were about to break into your house, where would you hide? What is the best hiding place in your house?

14

Some adults have a lot of trouble enjoying themselves. If you were asked to give them some advice about how to play and have more fun, what would you say?

15

Is there any particular moment in your past you wish had been captured on video? Would you like to have more videos and photos from when you were younger?

16

Who do you dislike the most? What is the best thing about that person?

17

Do you sometimes find yourself sitting in front of some awful-tasting food you're supposed to eat? If so, what's your best trick for getting rid of it without getting caught?

18

If you could be invisible for a day, what would you do?

19

When did you get yourself in the biggest mess by telling a lie? What do you think would have happened if you'd told the truth?

20

If you could choose any bedtime you wanted for the next year, what time would you pick?

21

Are there things you pretend not to like but really do enjoy—for example, being kissed by your parents or having a little sister tag along with you? If so, why do you hide your feelings?

22

When you're mad at your parents and want to get back at them, what's the best trick you have for getting on their nerves?

23

If you had to guess two things you'll like in a few years but don't like now, what would you guess? Pretend that if you are correct you will win $1,000.

24

If you could take either a pill that made you braver or one that made you stronger, which would you choose and why? Would you rather just stay as you are?

25

If you knew that by being the teacher's pet for two years you'd lose your friends and be teased by everyone, but later in life would be happy, successful, and admired by everyone, would you do it?

26

Do you think you have too many chores? If you could be the one to assign the chores in your house, what would you give yourself to do?

27

If your parents said they were going to have another baby and thought you were so terrific that they'd clone an identical twin of you, would you like or hate the idea? What do you think would be the worst thing about it? The best?

28

Would you rather your mom or dad gave you more presents or spent more time with you? Which would make you feel more loved?

29

If you were offered $250 to kiss someone you liked in front of your school class, would you do it?

30

If you had a dog you really loved, and a mean neighbor killed it just because it pooped on his lawn, what do you think should happen to the person?

31

What is the worst nightmare you can remember? Would you be willing to have the same dream tonight if you could spend a week at Disneyland with your friends?

32

If you woke up tomorrow and by magic were grown up and had kids of your own, how would you treat them differently than your parents treat you?

33

How would you feel if you found out today you were adopted as a baby? Would you try to find your biological parents?

34

If you agreed to sell your bike to a friend and someone later offered you more money, would you try to back out of the deal?

35

If you and your friends were collecting money for a charity, and your friends decided to steal what they were collecting and said they wouldn't be friends with you unless you joined them, what would you do?

36

If you could be as talented as some friend of yours at any one thing, what would you choose?

37

Would you rather wear the same uniform to school every day or wear anything you want? What would you wear if no one paid any attention to the way you dressed?

38

Clean your room! Take a bath! Wash your hands! Why do you think adults care so much about cleanliness?

39

If you told your friends everything about yourself, including the things you are most embarrassed of, do you think they'd like you less or more than they do now?

40

Are you in a hurry to grow up? What does it mean to be "grown up," and when do you think it will happen to you?

41

While on vacation, you go to the beach with a friend's parents and people there are bathing nude. Would you want to stay and watch or leave?

42

If everyone stopped growing and getting stronger when they reached your age, so adults were neither bigger nor stronger than you, would you still do what they said? If so, why?

43

If you had only five minutes to think up a nickname for yourself and knew everyone would use it for years, what would you pick? What name would you pick for your best friend? Your parents?

44

Imagine that your principal told you she wanted to make school better and would change it in any one way you suggested. What would you tell her to do?

45

Of all the things you've heard about God and religion, what do you think is true and what do you think might be just a story?

46

If you could permanently trade lives with one of your classmates, brothers, or sisters, would you? If so, who would you pick and why?

47

If you could change any one thing about your parents, what would it be?

48

What things do you think kids should be punished for, and how should it be done? Is there an age when people are too old to be punished for the mistakes they make? If so, what age and why?

49

What are you most proud of having done?
What would make you even prouder?

50

If everyone in your class but you would be killed unless you agreed to sacrifice your own life, would you save everyone else or save yourself? Would it matter if no one would ever know about what you had done?

51

What do you like most about your best friend? How long do you think it would take to make another "best" friend if you moved away?

52

Would you rather be very poor but have parents who loved you and each other, or be fabulously wealthy but have parents who ignored you and were always fighting with each other?

53

If someone pulled down a friend's pants at a movie theater, would you laugh along with everyone else?

54

What is the most boring thing you can imagine doing? Would you do it for a whole week if you could then celebrate your birthday twice each year?

55

What is the biggest difference between what happens on television and what happens in the real world?

56

Is there anyone you trust so much that you wouldn't be afraid to have him or her know every single thought you have?

Would you be willing to never again get any gifts and surprises if instead you could just ask for anything you wanted and have your parents immediately buy it for you?

58

What makes you feel guilty? Do people try to make you feel guilty very often?

59

If someone a lot smaller than you kept teasing you and telling lies about you and wouldn't stop, how far would you be willing to go to make the person stop? What about someone bigger than you?

60

Have you ever thought you were going to die—for example, in a big thunderstorm or a car accident? If so, did the experience teach you anything you could tell your friends?

61

When was the last time you were so mad at a friend that you screamed? Do you think you get over your anger more quickly when you show how mad you are or when you hide it?

62

Which subjects at school do you think will be completely useless when you get older? Which ones do you think will be important?

63

Would you spend two days all alone in your house if you knew nothing bad would happen and you could have any present you wanted afterwards?

64

When was the last time you told your parents you loved them? When was the last time they told you?

65

Are there certain kinds of stealing—or borrowing without permission—that are all right and others that aren't? If so, what is the difference between them? When was the last time you stole something or thought about stealing something?

66

What is the hardest thing about growing up?

67

When someone says you are just like your mom or dad, do you like it? Do you try to be more like your parents or to be different from them?

68

Would you rather hang around with a group of younger kids and be the boss but do things younger kids do, or hang around with a group of older kids and be the squirt but do things older kids get to do?

69

What was the most exciting thing you ever did on a dare? Are you glad or sorry you did it?

70

Would you eat a worm sandwich if you'd get to be on your favorite TV show or meet your favorite movie star or musician?

71

Would you like your parents to cuddle and hug each other more or less than they do now? What about having them hug and kiss you more or less than now?

If you found a purse or wallet on the playground with a lot of money in it, and no one saw you pick it up, what would you do?

73

If you could take a pill that made you sore for a week, but kept you healthy for an extra ten years when you got old, would you want it? Would you change your mind if it didn't make you sick or if it made you really sick for a whole month?

Is there any argument you have again
and again with your dad or mom or
grandparents? If so, is there anything
you could do to prevent it? Do you
sometimes just enjoy arguing?

What's the luckiest thing that ever
happened to you?

If you liked someone who later turned out to be a liar, would you still want to be friends?

What advice would you give to a friend whose parents were getting a divorce and always trying to make him or her take sides in their arguments?

78

Did you ever stand up for something you thought was right even though a lot of people got upset with you? If not, do you think you could be strong enough to do so?

When you're at school, do you act like a different person than when you're with your family?

80

What things are too personal to discuss with your parents? Is there anyone you can talk to about these things?

81

Do you have many mementos, souvenirs, and photographs? If so, how much money would someone have to give you to get you to throw them all away?

82

What is something you love doing now but will probably not enjoy in two years?

83

On Halloween, a group of high-school students are caught scaring little kids and stealing their candy. If you could decide the punishment, what would it be?

84

Would you rather be a rich and famous movie star or a great doctor who saves a lot of people but is not wealthy or well known?

Have you ever seen your parents drunk or very ill? How did it feel to see them that way?

Of all the nice things someone could truthfully say about you, which one would make you feel best?

87

What is the worst word you know? How did you learn it and when was the last time you said it?

88

When is the last time you really laughed at yourself because you did something silly or stupid?

89

If you could have one of your friends do anything you wanted and be your slave for a day, what would you ask for? Pretend he or she wouldn't get upset no matter what it was.

90

If you could make your parents try any one food, what would it be? Do you think kids should be forced to try new foods?

91

If this Saturday you could do absolutely anything in the world you wanted, what would you do?

92

Who is your biggest hero? Why do you think this person is so terrific?

93

When was the last time you lied to your parents? To a close friend? When was the last time you got caught lying?

94

What tricks do your friends use to get you to do things they know you don't want to do?

95

Do you pick your nose or bite your nails? If so, do you think you always will, or will you stop one day?

96

What, if anything, have adults told you that you think might not be true? Do you think they actually believed what they were saying?

97

If you could change any one thing about the way you look, what would it be?

98

If your pet needed an expensive operation and could have it only if you agreed to give up Christmas and birthday presents for two years, would you do it?

99

Are you afraid to ask questions when you don't understand something? For example, do you sometimes fake a laugh when you don't understand a joke?

100

What is the best costume you ever wore? Would you like getting dressed up in costumes every week if you could?

101

Have you and your friends ever picked on people and made fun of them until they cried? If so, why did you do it? Did you enjoy it?

102

Are there things your parents won't do, but still make you do because it's supposed to be "good for you"? If so, do you think this is fair?

103

If an older kid hit you, stole something of yours, and then said he'd hurt you if you told on him, would you tell anyone? If so, who?

104

Are you more likely to hold back your tears when you feel like crying or to hold back your laughter when you see something funny? Why?

105

Do you wish your parents would question you less or more about what you do and how you feel?

106

If your parents told you your best friend was no good and you couldn't see him or her anymore, how would you feel? Would you do what they said?

107

Have you ever farted and blamed someone else for it?

If you knew you wouldn't get caught, would you cheat on a test by copying someone's answers? What would you think if you saw other people cheating?

When was the last time you did something for a stranger just to be nice?

110

If it would save the lives of ten kids in another country, would you be willing to have really bad acne for a year? What about not getting any new clothes for a year?

111

If you knew your best friend had stolen something from a neighbor, and your father asked you what you knew about it, would you lie to protect your friend?

112

If you knew that by practicing hard every Saturday you could become the best in your school at whatever you wanted, what—if anything—would you work on? Imagine it is twenty years from now and you are looking back on the choice you just made. Do you think you'd wish you had picked something else to work on?

113

What is your biggest fear? How would your life be different if suddenly you weren't afraid of this anymore?

114

If your parents lost their jobs and you had to try to help support your family, what would you do to earn money?

115

If you could pick any one food and have as much of it as you wanted—but nothing else—during the next week, what would you pick?

What would make you try harder in school: wanting to please a teacher you liked, not wanting to disappoint your parents, or being offered a fabulous prize if you did well?

117

How important is it for you to win? When was the last time you cheated in a game so you could win?

118

If you got so angry at your parents that you decided to run away, where would you go? If you ran away, do you think you'd ever come home again?

119

If there was a hard but exciting project to do, would you rather do it by yourself and get all the credit, or work with your friends knowing that everyone would share the credit? What would it feel like to do it the other way?

120

What's the most embarrassing thing that ever happened to you? Are you embarrassed now by the same things that used to embarrass you?

Whose room would you most like to spend the afternoon looking through? Pretend you had permission to look at all the private possessions there.

122

Would it be worse to have to stay in your room for a week with a phone, computer, and TV, or to be able to go anywhere you want but have all electronic devices be off-limits?

123

Do your parents try to trick you into doing things? If so, do you usually figure out what's going on right away or not until later?

If you could grow up to be famous and successful, what would you like to be known for? Do you think you'll be famous someday?

If you had to either always rush and do things a lot more quickly than you do now, or always take your time and do things a lot more slowly than you do now, which would you prefer? Does it bother you more to be around people who are much faster or much slower than you are?

126

If you could do one thing you're not allowed to do now because you're supposedly too young, what would it be?

When were you last in a fight? What would you be willing to fight about that doesn't directly threaten you?

If you could choose to be the most attractive, the most athletic, or the smartest kid in your school, which would you want to be?

What do you think your parents worried about when they were your age? What do you think they worry about now?

If you could have any one magical power, what would you pick?

If a friend tried to show you a place on the Internet where there were lots of dirty pictures, would you look at them?

132

If you could take a genetic test to discover what things you'd be best at, would you want to take it or just find out for yourself over time?

133

If you could have either a wonderful new experience or a wonderful new possession, which would you want? Why?

134

If suddenly television was going to have either all sex or all violence removed, but not both, which one would you rather see disappear? Why?

135

What kinds of teasing do you think you'd miss most if everyone agreed to never tease you again?

136

What do you think your friends like most about you? If you lost that quality, do you think they'd still like you?

137

Adults can do more, but they have more responsibilities. Children can play more, but they get told what to do. Do you think kids or adults have a better deal?

138

If you could make a TV show about anything you wanted and knew that millions of people would see it, what would it be about?

139

Would you rather have a job you didn't like that paid a lot or a job you loved that paid just enough to get by on?

140

If you could see into the future but not change anything, would you want to take a look?

141

What is the wildest and craziest thing you've ever done? Would you like to do it again?

142

Have you ever gotten yourself into a mess by telling people you could do things you really couldn't?

143

If your two best friends got so mad at each other that they both refused to come to your birthday party if the other one was going to be there, what would you do?

144

If you were mad at your brother and found out about something bad he'd done, would you tell your parents and get him in trouble?

145

Would you like to have a watch with a HELP button you could press to immediately summon the police anytime you were in danger? Can you think of a time you would really have liked to have something like that?

146

If one morning you woke up and found that during the night you'd been magically transformed into an adult, what would you do? Pretend you know you will become a kid again in one week.

147

If your principal decided to put tiny video cameras in all the classrooms so parents could go to the Internet anytime and watch their kids, would the idea bother you? How would having cameras like that everywhere change the way you feel about school?

148

If you could somehow make any one person in the world absolutely adore you, who would you pick? Does anyone like you now who you wish didn't?

149

If you couldn't watch TV for a year, what do you think you'd do with all the extra time? Do you think you'd be better off if you got to watch more TV than you do now, or if you had to watch less of it? Why?

150

Are you worried about what kind of place the world will be when you grow up? If so, what worries you most and what do you think could be done to improve things?

151

If you knew that by cheating you could win an important competition for your school and be a hero, would you? Pretend you were sure you wouldn't get caught.

152

If you could gain the ability either to talk to animals or see the future, which would you want?

153

If you could have anyone you know as a best friend, who would you pick?

154

If everyone in your class began teasing and picking on your best friend, and you knew that if you stayed friends everyone would start picking on you too, what would you do?

155

How would it make you feel if most people thought you were two years younger than you are? Two years older?

156

What do you think your parents should do for you without expecting to be thanked—for example, cooking your meals, buying your clothes, or taking you places? Do you think they would agree with you about this?

157

Have you had any personal experiences that lead you to believe in God? If so, why do you think there are so many people who haven't had such experiences? If not, why do you think so many other people have had them?

158

What is the best trick you ever played on someone?

159

If terrorists kidnapped some kids in your school and threatened to kill them unless the president released other terrorists from prison, would you ask him to save your classmates by freeing the terrorists? What if the ones in prison had murdered your favorite neighbor?

160

If your parents didn't care whether you got good grades or not, would it upset you? What do you know more about than the kid who gets the best grades in your class?

161

What advice would you give a good friend who got very jealous of someone and started trying to act just like that person?

162

At what age should kids be able to wear whatever they want to school? At what age should they be allowed to go on dates by themselves?

163

What grade would you give your teacher for the overall job she does? For her patience? For her friendliness? For her handwriting?

164

How do you feel when you see someone who is disfigured or disabled? Could you be best friends with someone extremely ugly?

165

Why do you think the most popular kids in school are so popular? In what ways do you think you are better than they are?

166

Is there anything so bad that if you found out your mother or father had done it, you'd call the police?

167

Do you try to act like your friends more than they try to act like you? Why?

168

Do you usually say what you really think or what you think other people want to hear? Do you think your life would be better or worse if you acted the other way more often?

169

Pretend you can own only one pair of shoes and have to choose between a pair that looks funny but feels great and one that looks terrific but feels lousy. Which would you pick?

If a rich kid wanted to buy your parents, how much would you ask for them—assuming you were willing to sell? Would you trade parents with any of your friends?

What's the best birthday party you ever had? If you could have any kind of party you wanted for your next birthday, what would you choose?

172

If you were riding your bicycle and accidentally ran into someone else's bike and wrecked it—but no one saw you— what would you do?

173

Have you ever been humiliated by a teacher? If so, what happened?

174

Would you rather be a bed wetter, but have only your parents know about it, or never wet your bed but, because of a story someone made up about you, have everyone think you did?

175

Would it be worse to spend a night all alone in an empty house in the woods, or to spend it with a friend outdoors in a violent thunderstorm?

176

If you had a chance to give a ten-minute speech to your whole school about anything you wanted, would you want to do it? What would you talk about?

177

What were you afraid of a few years ago that no longer bothers you?

178

If you were given $1,000 to use to help other people, how would you spend it?

179

Would you rather have more brothers and sisters than you have now or fewer? What do you think is the best size for a family? Why?

Do you think that when you grow up your parents will look at you and think you did better than they'd hoped you would or not as well?

Of all the things you could imagine doing when you grow up, what would most please your parents? What would most disappoint them?

182

Would you rather your family loved one another and always showed how they felt—sometimes fighting and yelling, sometimes hugging and kissing—or would you prefer they loved one another but hid their feelings when they got upset?

183

If you could have your room clean and neat all the time or jumbled and messy, which would you choose?

184

What things scare you even though you know there is no reason to be afraid?

185

Have you ever—without telling anyone— let someone beat you at a game you could easily have won? If so, why?

186

Can you remember a time you succeeded when you thought you never would? If so, how did it feel? Would you rather try ambitious things, knowing you might fail, or easier things you'll almost certainly succeed at?

If you had to pick an age to be for your whole life, knowing you'd never grow older, what age would you pick?

188

If you were a teacher and the kids in your class wouldn't listen to you, what would you do? What if they still wouldn't listen?

189

If two kids in your class were caught bringing a gun or a knife into school and you had to determine their punishment, what would you choose? Would it matter if one of them was a friend?

190

If you could live someone else's life for a week—just to see what it was like— would you want to? If so, who would it be and why?

191

If a good friend came to your house with a black eye and—after you promised to keep it secret—told you his father had hit him, would you tell anyone? What if you didn't, and two months later the same thing happened again?

192

When was the last time you felt completely happy? What made you feel so good?

If your baby-sitter said she'd let you stay up way past your bedtime if you promised not to tell anyone, would you agree? If you did, what would you say the next morning when your mother asked if you went to bed on time?

194

What's the worst accident you ever caused? Were you angrier at yourself than other people were, or was it the other way around?

195

What's your favorite daydream?

196

Have you ever been blamed for something you didn't do, yet not told on the person who really did it? If so, why didn't you tell?

If you could e-mail any famous person and be sure they'd read and answer your note, who would you write to and what would you say?

198

What are the stupidest rules your parents have about what you must and must not do? What's so stupid about these rules?

199

If for one day you could do anything you wanted and not get punished no matter what it was, what would you do?

200

If you had to pick a new first name for yourself, what would you choose?

If eating nothing but a tasteless food paste for a year would make you much stronger and more attractive, would you do it?

If a friend gave you a gift you didn't like, would you pretend you liked it?

Who is meanest to the kids in your neighborhood? If you knew you could get away with it, what trick would you play on him or her this Halloween? If you had to make up a story about how that person got to be so mean, what do you think it would be?

204

What was your biggest failure?

205

If a friend threw a party and didn't invite you, what would you do?

206

Would you rather be average in height or the tallest in your class?

207

If you could go to a special hi-tech summer program that was really hard but helped you do a lot better in school, would you want to go? Would you rather just take a pill that made you smarter?

208

What do you think your family would miss the most about you if you were to die? What would you miss most about them if they died?

Do you believe in God? If not, why do you think so many people do? If so, what do you think God does all day?

If you could set your own allowance, how much would it be? Why did you pick that amount?

After being given a truth pill, you are asked to describe each person in your family. What do you say?

212

If you could gaze into a magic mirror and see exactly what's happening anywhere in the world, where would you look and what do you think you'd see?

If your teacher and your mother spent an afternoon discussing you, would you like to secretly listen in on their conversation? What do you think they would say?

Have you ever wished someone would die—or have bad things happen to them? If so, who and why?

215

Would you rather have to repeat a grade in school or gain a lot of weight?

Have you ever seen your mom or dad cry? If not, how do you think it would feel to see that?

217

What's the best thing that could happen to you? The worst thing?

218

What do you most dislike about yourself?
Do you think other people care about it
as much as you do?

219

When you and your friends play together,
do you prefer being at your house or
theirs? Why?

220

If you were going to be stranded for ten years on a tiny island paradise the size of a football field, who would you want with you? Make believe you'd be in no danger and would have clothing, food, and shelter, but nothing else.

221

What things do you see people doing just to pass the time and keep busy? What do you do just to pass the time?

If you could be the star of a reality TV show that followed your family around the clock for a year, would you want to? Imagine that you would be a big celebrity, but that everyone would know everything about you and your family.

Who is your best friend? What is the worst thing about him or her?

224

Would you rather change out of a wet bathing suit in a crowded locker room, or wait to change at home an hour later?

225

If you could stop going to school, would you? What's the worst thing about school? What's the best?

Do you think it's fun to be a parent? If so, what do you think is the best thing about it? If not, why do you think people have kids?

If you were to give your mom and dad one tip on how to be better parents, what would you tell them?

What's the bravest thing you ever did?

229

If you were in a terrible auto accident and were dying, would you want your parents to donate your heart and other organs to save people's lives, even though the doctors would be cutting up your body?

If you bought something in a store and got a dollar too much back in change, would you say anything?

If something happened to your parents and you had to go live with someone else for two years, who would you want to stay with?

What, if anything, about your family would you be afraid to have your friends find out?

Is there any question you would be afraid to ask someone because of the answer you might get?

If a teacher wanted to find out what you really thought and felt, how could he or she best get you to open up?

235

Do adults ever try to get you to watch TV so you won't bother them? If so, how does that make you feel? Would you do the same thing if you were baby-sitting or had kids of your own?

236

If a friend's mother died in an accident, what would you say or do to try to comfort your friend? What, if anything, could you tell him or her about death?

How do you think your life would be different if you were three inches taller? Three inches shorter?

238

Has anyone done something so bad to you that you'd still like to get back at them if you could? What would you want to do to them?

239

Would it embarrass you to cry in front of your friends? Your father? Your little sister? If so, which would be worse and why?

240

If next year you could go to any school you wanted, would you want to go somewhere different? If so, how do you think it would be better there?

241

If friends of your parents served food that tasted disgusting and asked you how you liked it, what would you say? What do you think your parents would want you to say?

242

How do you think your life would change if someone in your family got really sick and had to stay in the hospital for a very long time?

243

If you had lots of money and could use it any way you wanted, what would you do with it?

244

Pretend that three people in a hospital are dying: a one-year-old baby, a grandmother with lots of grandchildren who love her, and a teenager who works hard but just flunked out of high school. If you could save only one of them, which would it be?

245

What do your parents do that most embarrasses you?

246

What foreign country have you heard the most about? What do you think it would be like to grow up there?

247

What really gets on your nerves?

248

What is one of your best tricks for getting attention from your parents? From your friends?

249

Would you like to have a brother who was just about the best brother you could imagine—friendly, smart, good at everything he tried, and close to you—if it meant that everyone would always talk about how great he was and not pay much attention to you?

250

Would you rather be slender and athletic but kind of dumb, or fat and clumsy but really smart?

Would you rather receive a gift you really wanted, or give your mother a gift she'd absolutely treasure?

There are lots of scary things in the world these days. What most worries you? What would you do if your fears came true?

253

Would you rather have no rules at all or live with the rules you have? If there weren't any rules, what would you do differently?

254

If another kid does something wrong, are you more inclined to tell an adult, ignore it, or try to solve the problem on your own? For example, if you saw someone stealing things, would you tell a teacher? What would you do if a big kid spit on your lunch?

If you knew that by never again eating junk foods or candy, you'd live to be eighty-five years old rather than seventy-five, would want to you give those treats up?

If you had a tiny camera recorder the size of a penny that could fly by remote control and be your spy, who and what— if anything—would you spy on?

257

If you could decide right now whether or not you will smoke cigarettes when you grow up, what would you decide? What about using drugs or drinking a lot? How do you think it would change your life if you did the opposite?

What is the scariest thing you've seen on a film or video game? Do you wish your parents had kept you from seeing it? Or would you like to see something even scarier?

What, if anything, do you think should be done to a kid caught illegally downloading lots of music and videos from the Web? Would your answer be different if he or she were selling copies to friends?

260

If your parents wanted everyone in the family to wear little monitor watches that would let any of you listen in on each other anytime you wanted, would you be willing to try this out for a year? How do you think it might change your family? Would you rather do this with your best friend instead?

261

When was the last time you laughed so hard you cried? If you could watch a movie that was so funny it made you laugh that hard for two whole hours, would you want to?

262

What is the most unfair thing about the way your family is run?

263

If you had the power to choose someone and always be able to read his or her mind, who would you pick?

264

What is the most important lesson you've learned about life in the past few years? How did you learn it?

265

What's the funniest story you ever made up about why you weren't able to get your homework finished on time? Did anyone actually believe you?

266

If drinking a magic potion would make you never again feel sad no matter what happened, would you drink it?

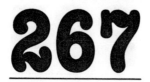

267

Pretend that right now you have to pick the job you will have as an adult. What's the best job you can think of? What's the worst?

268

If for an hour you could ask your parents any questions you wanted and knew they'd tell you the absolute unvarnished truth, what would you ask? Pretend they'd answer every question and then forget they'd even talked to you.

Gregory Stock started asking questions as a child and has continued to do so in his books, including the bestselling *Book of Questions,* which has sold 2 million copies and has been translated into 17 languages. Dr. Stock received a Ph.D. in biophysics from Johns Hopkins in 1977 and an MBA from Harvard in 1987. He now directs the program on Medicine, Technology and Society at UCLA and runs Signum Biosciences, a biotech company developing therapeutics for Alzheimer's disease. Dr. Stock regularly appears on radio and TV to debate the social, political, and policy implications of new technologies, particularly in genetics and reproductive medicine, the focus of several of his books. And he loves to ask questions that have no easy answers. He has one child.